The Lamentation of a Sinner

By

Queen Katherine Parr

With an Introduction by
Pastor Don Matzat

Good News Books
O'Fallon, Missouri
Copyright@ 2017 Donald G. Matzat

Dedicated to the memory of
Queen Katherine Parr of England
Who unashamedly was willing
To accuse herself before God and man
And find in Christ Jesus, through
"The Book of the Crucifix,"
Her life, identity, peace and joy.

Table of Contents

Introduction

Katherine Parr was the sixth and final wife of King Henry VIII. This treatise, therefore, *The Lamentation of a Sinner,* a profound confession of sin, remorse, repentance and faith, is not the work of some unknown personage, but rather of the Queen of England, lending both controversy and credibility: controversy, because it would have been deemed improper for a woman of such high standing to so abase herself, and credibility, because, if her alternative relationship with Christ was not authentic, why would she do it? It is, in my humble estimate, one of the more important, yet largely unknown, works to emerge out of the sixteenth century Protestant Reformation.

The reign of King Henry VIII of England (1509-1547), of the house of Tudor, could be appropriately described in the words of Charles Dickens, "It was the best of times. It was the worst of times." "Best of times" perhaps because of the eventual launch of the Protestant Reformation in England and the establishment of the Monarchy as head of the Church of England, thereby terminating Papal dominance; and "worst of times" because of the way the same was accomplished. It is incredulous to think that such momentous historical events were initiated because of the unrequited lust of King Henry. Indeed, God works in mysterious ways.

I am embarrassed to admit that my initial interest in the reign of Henry VIII and his six wives did not commence as an academic pursuit but rather as the result of viewing the oft obscene and at times fictional, yet well produced *Showtime* television presentation of the *The Tudors.* If one can get past the gratuitous nudity, the *The Tudors* offers an excellent adaptation of life in the court of King Henry VIII. I initially prided myself in the ability to name in order the six wives of Henry VIII, which impressed very few, nor should it have. Yet, it piqued my interest and resulted in much further study.

Perhaps, in the interest of putting *The Lamentation of a Sinner,* the work of Katherine Parr, into context, a very brief history of Henry's reign is in order.

Following the death of his father, Henry VII, Henry ascended the throne as the eighth due to the untimely death of his older brother Arthur, who was first in succession. At an early age, Arthur was officially betrothed to Catherine of Aragon, the daughter of Isabella and Ferdinand of Spain. They married in 1501, but Arthur died five months later. After the coronation of Henry VIII he immediately announced that he would marry Catherine, claiming that it was the wish of his father. They were married in 1509.

After numerous miscarriages and the birth of a son Henry who died seven weeks later, Catherine gave birth to a daughter Mary, who, as later events unfolded, would become Queen Mary I, otherwise known as "bloody Mary."

After having numerous affairs and becoming increasingly disenchanted with Catherine since she was seemingly unable to bear a male heir, Henry fell helplessly in love (or lust) with Anne Boleyn who was in the service of Queen Catherine. But Anne refused to yield herself to Henry's desires and be his mistress, only promising such favors after they were married, causing the King much frustration. This set-in motion Henry's quest to have his marriage to Catherine annulled and be free to marry Anne. He claimed it had not been proper for him to marry his brother's wife.[1]

Since the Pope refused to grant an annulment, Henry, after much machination, declared himself to

---

[1] Martin Luther weighed in on this subject. He wrote, "Under no circumstances will he be free to divorce the Queen to whom he is married, the wife of his deceased brother, and thus make the mother as well as the daughter into incestuous women. Even if the King might have sinned by marrying the wife of his deceased brother, and even if the dispensation granted by the Roman pope might not have been valid (I do not debate this now), nevertheless it would be a heavier and more dreadful sin [for the King] to divorce the woman he had married; and this especially why then the King, as well as the Queen and the Young Queen, could be forever charged with, and considered as, being incestuous people. According to my opinion, therefore, those who urge the King to the divorce for this reason alone torture his conscience in vain. If he has sinned by marrying, then this sin is past, and like all other sins of the past is amended through repentance; but the marriage should not be torn apart for this reason, and such a heavy future sin ought not to be permitted." Luther, M. (1999, c1975). *Luther's Works*, vol. 50: Letters III, Pages 32-33, Philadelphia: Fortress Press.

be the head of the Church of England, giving him the authority to annul his own marriage of twenty-four years to Catherine of Aragon. He married Anne Boleyn in a secret ceremony. The newly appointed Archbishop of Canterbury, Thomas Cranmer, declared Henry and Catherine's marriage null and void; and Henry and Anne's marriage valid. Shortly afterwards, the Pope excommunicated both Cranmer and Henry. The break with Rome was finalized. Henry and Anne were officially married in a public ceremony in 1533.

Anne bore Henry one child, another daughter, Elizabeth, who again, as future events unfolded, would succeed her half-sister Mary to the throne as Elizabeth I, the "Virgin Queen," ushering in the "Elizabethan Era" in English history, but also ending the Tudor dynasty.

Henry also soon became disenchanted with Anne and her failure to produce a male heir. He began courting Jane Seymour, who had been Queen Catherine's maid of honor and was in service to Queen Anne. Accusations were raised about the fidelity of Queen Anne, her former affairs and possible incest. She was tried and arrested for treason and beheaded. Henry married Jane Seymour soon thereafter.

Queen Jane gave birth to Edward, King Henry's sole male heir who would succeed him to the throne, but in childbirth, Jane Seymour died. She was the only one of Henry's wives to be granted a queen's funeral.

Thomas Cromwell, King Henry's chief advisor, urged the King to marry German born Anne of Cleaves, possibly with the hope of aligning England with the Lutheran Reformation. After viewing a painting of Anne which, in our day we might conclude was "photoshopped," Henry agreed to the marriage, but upon meeting Anne was sorely disappointed by her appearance. He reluctantly married her but the marriage was never consummated and declared null and void. Because of his bad advice and trickery, Thomas Cromwell was accused of treason and beheaded. Anne remained in England and was favorably treated.

Henry had already begun an affair with seventeen-year-old Catherine Howard. After his marriage to Anne of Cleaves was terminated, he married young Catherine, but she was not thrilled with having a singular relationship with this elderly, obese King and sought young lovers. She was caught in her infidelity, accused of treason, and beheaded.

So, after much tribulation, deception and tragic consequences, this brings us to our main character, the next in line for Henry's final marital pursuit, Katherine Parr.

Katherine, a woman of means, who had been married and widowed twice before, attended the court of King Henry for the singular purpose of being close to the man she loved, Sir Thomas Seymour, the brother of former Queen Jane Seymour. She caught the eye of the King, who subsequently eliminated the competition of Seymour by assigning

11

him to a position in Brussels and proposed marriage to Katherine. She accepted Henry's proposal, possibly out of a sense of duty, or fear, or perhaps the hope of influencing the religious views of the King. They were married in 1543 and Katherine became Queen of England.

Although brought up in the Catholic faith, which in *The Lamentation* she brutally rebuked, speaking of "Papal riffraff," she became interested in and finally fully embraced the teachings of the Protestant Reformation. In 1545, she published her first book, *Prayers or Meditations*, the first book published by a woman in England under her own name and in the English language. Eventually, the Queen's religious beliefs were viewed with suspicion by the conservative anti-Protestant officials Stephen Gardiner, the Bishop of Winchester and Lord Chancellor Thomas Wriothesley (pronounced Risley).

Because Henry had established himself as the head of the Church of England and rejected the authority of the Pope did not mean that he subsequently rejected Roman Catholic doctrine. England was by and large a Catholic country, although elements of the Reformation were popularly held and initially tolerated. Henry appointed Thomas Cromwell, a proponent of the Reformation, as his chief minister replacing the infamous Cardinal Wolsey and Thomas Cranmer, who would eventually give Protestant substance to the Church of England, as the Archbishop of

Canterbury. He also allowed the Bible[2] to be translated into English and made available in every parish. Yet doctrinal confusion existed.

In 1539, Henry reversed his course. *The Act of Six Articles* returned the Church to Catholic orthodoxy, minus papal supremacy. The Catholic doctrine of transubstantiation, the bread and wine in the Sacrament is in substance the body and blood of Christ, was reaffirmed. Clerical marriage was condemned. This was an embarrassment to the Archbishop of Canterbury, Thomas Cranmer, whose marriage was an open secret at the time. He moved his wife and children out of England to safety.

More significantly, under this act, heresy again became a felony. It was clear that Henry VIII would not tolerate those with radical Protestant religious views. Protestants were punished for violating the *Six Articles*, while Catholics were punished for denying the royal supremacy over the church.

There had been efforts on the part of Cromwell and Cranmer to align the doctrine of the English Church with the German Reformation. Dialogue took place. But Henry wasn't interested. He refused to accept justification by faith, denying the salvific efficacy of good works. Luther considered Henry a lost cause and wrote: "Perhaps God does not wish

---

[2] *The Great Bible* of 1539, so designated because of its immense size, was the first authorized edition of the Bible in English, authorized by King Henry VIII. to be read aloud in the church services of the Church of England. The Great Bible was prepared by Myles Coverdale, working under commission of Thomas Cromwell.

his gospel to be touted by this King who has such a bad reputation."[3]

In 1545, Anne Askew, a devout Protestant left her home and family in Lincolnshire (or was thrown out by her Catholic husband whom she intended to divorce) and moved to London to promote her Protestant views. She vehemently attacked the Catholic doctrine of transubstantiation. She was arrested for heresy and suspected of influencing Queen Katherine. Under torture, she refused to implicate the Queen. Anne Askew was burned at the stake as a heretic in 1546.

Gardiner and Wriothesley continued to be suspicious of Katherine especially since she had the King's ear and often engaged in theological dialogue with him, promoting her Lutheran ideas which, of course, was potentially perilous. They convinced Henry of her heresy. With his approval, an arrest warrant was issued against her. She was informed, surreptitiously, that such a warrant was to be executed the following day

That night, she attempted to placate Henry by humbling herself before him, acknowledging his superior theological knowledge, debasing her feminine insights, and assuring him that the only reason she discussed controversial Protestant teaching with him was so that she could learn from him. She succeeded.

---

[3] Luther, M. (1999, c1975). Vol. 50: Luther's works, vol. 50: Letters III (J. J. Pelikan, H. C. Oswald & H. T. Lehmann, Ed.). Luther's Works (Vol. 50, Page 203). Philadelphia: Fortress Press.

The next morning, the King and Queen were in the garden when Lord Wriothesley together with armed guards approached to arrest the Queen. Henry severely rebuked them and sent them away. There would be no further conflict between Henry and Katherine.

King Henry VIII died January 28, 1547 at the age of 55. Thomas Cranmer was at his bedside, holding his hand, and reciting evangelical teaching, acknowledging the all-sufficient atoning work of Christ, rather than offering him last rites. He was entombed alongside Jane Seymour.

It is evident that Katherine wrote *The Lamentation of a Sinner* in 1546 while Henry was still alive. She speaks highly of the King, comparing him with Moses who overthrew Pharaoh in the same way the King had vanquished the Pope. Yet, she did not publish the treatise until November of 1547 after the King's death and during the reign of young Edward VI, at which time, primarily through his advisors, Protestantism was firmly entrenched in the land, and Catholics were persecuted. If the treatise had been published before the death of Henry, Katherine would have most certainly joined Anne Askew at the stake.

After the death of Henry, Katherine Parr married her old love Thomas Seymour. She died in 1548 at the age of 35 after giving birth to her only child, Mary Seymour. Throughout her life, her motto was "To be useful in all that I do." She is entombed at Sudeley Castle in Gloucestershire.

Of course, this was not the end of the religious turmoil in England. After Edward died at the age of 15, Queen Mary I, the Roman Catholic daughter of Catherine of Aragon ascended the throne and re-established Catholicism in the land, burning 280 dissenters at the stake, thus gaining the name of "bloody Mary." After her five-year reign terminated by death, she was succeeded by her half-sister, Protestant Elizabeth I, daughter of Anne Boleyn, who reversed her policies. She established the Protestant Church of England and repealed the heresy laws, promoting religious toleration. She reigned for 44 years and England mainly flourished during the "Elizabethan Era."

My interest in the treatise *The Lamentation of a Sinner* is neither literary nor historical but theological. In my theological musings, I have often contemplated the relationship between self-accusation and hearing the Good News of forgiveness and justification. Martin Luther often spoke of the relationship between the two and said, "The righteous man is one who accuses himself first"[4]

Merely by chance I came upon a reference to this treatise in *Wikipedia*. The article stated that *The Lamentation of a Sinner* by Katherine Parr contained an unusual degree of self-debasement that would not have been appropriate for the monarch's wife

---

[4] Luther, M. (1999, c1974). Vol. 10: Luther's works, vol. 10: First Lectures on the Psalms I: Psalms 1-75 (J. J. Pelikan, H. C. Oswald & H. T. Lehmann, Ed.). Luther's Works (Ps 2:9). Saint Louis: Concordia Publishing House.

and promoted the Lutheran concept of justification by faith alone. I thought, "I need to read this!"

It was one thing for the average person, of whatever degree or position he or she may have attained, to be confronted with the Law of God and engage in confession and self-accusation as a prelude to hearing the Gospel. But this was the Queen of England accusing and abasing herself to gain Christ! But the treatise was nowhere to be found, even though it was obviously old enough to be in the public domain.

In searching *Amazon* for books written about the life and writing of Katherine Parr, I discovered a massive work titled *Katherine Parr; Complete Works and Correspondence* edited by Dr. Janel Mueller, Distinguished Service Professor and Dean Emerita, English and Humanities, The University of Chicago. It contained the treatise.

I ordered the book, anticipated its arrival and read the treatise with great joy. I was amazed that this woman, Katherine Parr, who had arrived at such a lofty estate, would so debase herself to find her life in the person of Jesus Christ.

By and large her theology was sound. I was particularly impressed by her understanding of the sole function of faith as "apprehending" the grace of God, making a very clear distinction between a "living faith" and mere historical knowledge. At times, she did seem to present a Calvinist view of election and perhaps placed an excessive emphasis on feeling and emotion.

One issue I found particularly interesting was her desire for "prevenient grace," or "grace that came before." She emphasized praying for the Holy Spirit to open her eyes to truth rather than simply trusting the Gospel as the vehicle for that grace. While the subject of prevenient grace received a full treatment in Wesley's Methodism, it was also a part of Roman Catholic theology and confirmed at the Council of Trent. Yet it is very evident that her praying for the Holy Spirit and seeking the "grace that came before," was not divorced from the objective sureties of the Word of God, since her treatise is replete with biblical, Gospel references.

I felt compelled to self-publish this treatise as a small, stand-alone volume. Since Dr. Mueller had updated the ancient English used by Queen Katherine into an Elizabethan style or, if you will, "King James speak," I wanted to take it a step further, and hopefully put it into English the average person might readily understand.

The problem was, Dr. Mueller's adaptation was a derivative work and therefore copyrighted, so I required her permission to do so. I went to the University of Chicago website and found their faculty roster, including the name of Dr. Janel Mueller and her email address. I wrote to her, sharing my intention. I honestly did not expect a response, but I was wrong. She graciously gave me permission to adapt her version of *The Lamentation* and commented, "You have my best wishes as you continue your retirement projects."

If there are those and who wish to study the life, correspondence and writings of Katherine Parr in much greater detail, I highly recommend Dr. Mueller's scholarly work.

So, one of my "retirement projects" has been to edit, adapt and rewrite *The Lamentation of a Sinner* in a style that the average person would have no difficulty understanding. I attempted to do so with great care, not wanting in any way to do an injustice to Katherine's words and thoughts. Much of Dr. Mueller's adaptation remains mostly intact while some sections have been transliterated.

I had some difficulty trying to nail down the position of politician William Cecil in his *Prefatory Letter.* While he speaks of the value of the treatise, encouraging the reader to judge it based on its own merit, he makes it clear that his intention, because he cannot find adequate words, is not to get people to "like" it. Obviously, there would be numerous people, especially among the nobility, who prided themselves in their wealth or position, who would not "like" it.

There are many today who would not "like" *The Lamentation of a Sinner.* Those who are critical of the church's proclamation of the Law and the sinful human condition might refer to it as the promotion of "worm theology,"[5] while others would find it injurious to individual self-esteem.

---

[5] The term "worm theology" is attributed to a line in the Isaac Watts hymn *Alas! and Did My Savior Bleed,* which says "Would he devote that sacred head for such a worm as I?"

But, if you follow the example of Queen Katherine and lament your fallen state, and seeing yourself through the eyes of God, accuse yourself for the sake of gaining Christ, you will discover, with Queen Katherine, that you have gained abundantly more than you have given up.

So, I offer this work to you hopefully in a style you will be able to easily comprehend. Read and meditate upon the words of Queen Katherine. In his *Prefatory Letter,* William Cecil wrote: "These great mysteries and graces are not properly understood, except they be surely studied."

Dr. Donald G. Matzat
O'Fallon, Missouri, 2017

Don Matzat has been a pastor in the Lutheran Church-Missouri Synod for over fifty years. He has authored numerous books, including *Inner Healing: Deliverance or Deception, Christ-Esteem, Truly Transformed* and *The Lord Told Me, I Think* in addition to four novels.

Title Page

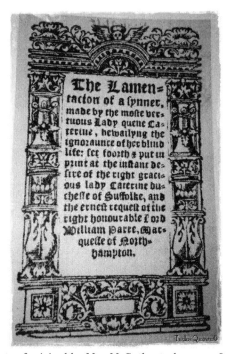

(Photo of original by Meg McGath - tudorqueen6.com)

The Lamentation of a Sinner

made by the most virtuous lady Queen Katherine, bewailing the ignorance of her blind life: set forth and put in print at the instant desire of the right gracious lady Katherine, Duchess of Suffolk, and the earnest request of the right honorable lord William Parr, Marquess of Northampton.

Prefatory Letter

William Cecil,[6] having taken much profit by the reading of this treatise, desires every Christian, by reading it, the same profit with increase from God.

Most gentle and Christian reader, if matters were confirmed by their reporters rather than the reports determined by the matters, I might justly lament our time, where evil deeds are described as good, and charitable deeds called evil. But since it is true that things are not good because they are praised, but rather, they are praised because they are good. It is not my intention to convince you to like this Christian treatise because I have chosen to praise it. But I urge you to consider it, for whatever goodness you shall ascribe to it. I am not writing to convince you to like this treatise, but to follow my example by passing judgment based on the treatise itself, not on what others say about it.

Truly our age is so disposed to use good words to describe evil fruits, and apply excellent terms to unkind works, so that charitable deeds cannot enjoy a proper description, being defrauded by the evil; and excellent works cannot be defined with worthy terms, being prevented by the unkind works. Men say as much as they can about a matter rather than how much they should say, inclining more to their own enjoyment rather than to their judgment. They

---

[6] William Cecil, 1st Baron Burghley (1520–1598) was an English statesman, the chief advisor of Queen Elizabeth I for most of her reign, twice Secretary of State (1550–53 and 1558–72) and Lord High Treasurer from 1572.

try to be eloquent regardless of whether the matter is good or evil, so that neither the goodness of the cause can move them to say more, nor the evilness less.

For if the excellency of this Christian contemplation, either for its marvelous goodness or for the resulting profit for the reader, should be commended, it would be necessary for me to find new words since the old ones have already been used to describe evil works, or I could wish that the common speech of praising was suspended until suitable matters were found to use them. Such is the abundance of praising, and scarceness of deserving. Wherefore, lacking the manner in words, and not indeed the matter of granting high commendation, I am compelled to be silent and not offer my judgment. I trust that those who might have been moved to like this treatise based on my judgment, will be compelled to grant it honor based upon its own worthiness.

Any earthly man would soon be stirred to see some mystery of magic, or practice of alchemy, or perchance some enchantment of elements,[7] but you, who are baptized, have here a wonderful mystery of the mercy of God, a heavenly practice of regeneration, a spiritual enchantment of the grace of God. If joy and triumphs are shown when a king's child is born to the world, what joy is sufficient when

---

[7] Perhaps a reference to the Roman Catholic teaching of transubstantiation where by the elements in the Sacrament are changed into the body and blood of Christ.

God's child is regenerated from heaven? The one is flesh, which is born of flesh; the other is spirit, which is born of spirit.[8] The one shall in brief time wither like the grass of the earth; the other shall live in heaven beyond all time. If the finding of one lost sheep be more joyful than having the ninety and nine, what joy is it to consider the return of a stray child of almighty God, whose return teaches the ninety and nine to come to their fold?[9] Even such cause of joy is this, that the angels in heaven take comfort herein. Be therefore, joyful where a noble child is newly born. Show thyself glad where the lost sheep has won the whole flock. Be not sad, where angels rejoice.

Here you may see one (if you are so moved) a woman, (if degree may aggravate you) a woman of high estate: by birth made noble, by marriage most noble, by wisdom godly; by a mighty King, an excellent Queen; by a famous Henry, a renowned Katherine. A wife to him that was a King to realms: refusing the world wherein she was lost, to obtain heaven, wherein she may be saved; abhorring sin, which made her bound, to receive grace, whereby she may be free; despising flesh, the cause of corruption, to put on the Spirit, the cause of sanctification; forsaking ignorance, wherein she was blind, to come to knowledge, whereby she may see; removing superstition, wherewith she was

---

[8] John 3:6
[9] Luke 15:7

smothered, to embrace true religion, wherewith she may revive.

The fruit of this treatise, good reader, is your own amendment; if only this, the writer is satisfied. This good lady thought no shame to detect her sin, to obtain remission; no vileness, to become nothing, to be a member of Him, which is all things in all; no folly to forget the wisdom of the world, to learn the simplicity of the Gospel; at the last, not being displeased to submit herself to the school of the cross, the learning of the crucifix, the book of our redemption, the very absolute library of God's mercy and wisdom. This way she thought her honor increased, and her state permanent: to make her earthly honor heavenly, and neglect the transitory for the everlasting. Of this, I would inform you, that profit may follow.

These great mysteries and graces are not properly understood, except they be surely studied; neither are they perfectly studied, unless they are diligently practiced; neither profitably practiced, without amending your life. See and learn what she has done: then may you practice, and amend what you can. So, shall you practice with ease, having a guide; and amend with profit, having a zeal. It is easier to see these than to merely learn them.

Begin at the easiest, to come to the harder. First, consider her confession, that you may learn her repentance; practice her perseverance, that you may have similar amendment; displease yourself in shunning vice, that you may please God in asking grace. Let not shame hinder your confession, which certainly did not hinder your sin. Be sure, if we acknowledge our sins, God is faithful to forgive us, and to cleanse us from all unrighteousness.[10] Obey the prophet's saying: "Declare thy ways to the Lord."[11] Thus far, you may learn to know yourself; but next, be as diligent to relieve yourself in God's mercy as you have been revealing yourself in your sin and repentance. For God has concluded all things under sin, so that He would have mercy upon all.[12] Who has also borne our sins in His body, upon the tree, that we should be delivered from sin, and should live to righteousness: by whose stripes we are healed.[13]

Here is our anchor; here is our Shepherd; here we are made whole. Here is our life, our redemption, our salvation, and our bliss. Let us, therefore, now feed by this gracious Queen's example; and do not be ashamed to become in confession publicans, since this noble lady will be no Pharisee. And to all ladies of estate I wish as earnest mind to follow our Queen in virtue as in honor: that they might once appear to prefer God before the world, and be honorable in religion, as you are now honorable in vanities. So, shall they (as in some virtuous ladies of right high estate it is viewed with great comfort) taste of this freedom of remission, of this everlasting bliss which exceeds all thoughts and understandings, and is prepared for the holy in

---

[10] 1 John1:9
[11] Psalm 37:5
[12] Galatians 3:22
[13] 1 Peter 2:24

spirit. For the which, let us, with our intercession in holiness and pureness of life, offer ourselves to the heavenly Father an undefiled host: to whom be eternal praise and glory, through all the earth, without end. Amen.

The Lamentation of a Sinner

Part One

When I think about my evil and wretched former life, my obstinate, stony, and exceedingly evil stubborn heart, I not only neglected, yes, but condemned and despised God's holy teachings and commandments, and embraced, received, and esteemed vain, foolish, and artificial trifles. Partly by the hate I owe to sin, which has reigned in me, and partly by the love I owe to all Christians, whom I am content to edify with the example of my own shame, I am forced and constrained with my heart and words to confess and declare to the world, how ingrate, negligent, unkind, and stubborn I have been to God my Creator; and how beneficial, merciful, and gentle He has always been to me, His creature, being such a miserable and wretched sinner.

Truly, I have undertaken no small thing: first, to set forth my whole stubbornness and contempt in words, which are incomprehensible in thought, as it is said in the Psalm: "Who understands his faults?"[14] Next, to declare the excellent benevolence, mercy, and goodness of God, which is infinite, unmeasurable. All the words of angels and men could not recount His exalted goodness. If one considers what he has received from God, and daily

---

[14] Psalm 19:12

31

receives, who is not forced to confess the same? Yes, if men would not acknowledge and confess the same, the stones would cry it out.[15] Truly, I am constrained and forced to speak and write of my own confusion and shame, but to the great glory and praise of God. For He, as a loving Father, of most abundant and exalted goodness, has heaped upon me innumerable blessings; and I, contrary, have heaped many sins, despising that which was good, holy, pleasant, and acceptable in His sight, and choosing that which was delicious, pleasant, and acceptable in my sight.

And it was no marvel that I did so. For I would not learn to know the Lord and His ways, but loved darkness better than light:[16] yes, darkness seemed to me, light. I embraced ignorance as perfect knowledge; and knowledge seemed to me superfluous and vain. I had little regard for God's Word, but gave myself to vanities and shadows of the world. I forsook Him, in whom is all truth, and followed the vain, foolish imaginations of my own heart. I covered my sins with the pretense of holiness. I called superstition, "godly meaning," and true holiness, "error."

The Lord did speak many pleasant and sweet words to me, and I would not hear. He called me in many ways, but through rebellion, I would not answer. My evils and miseries are so many and so great, they accuse me even to my face. Oh, how

---

[15] Luke 19:40
[16] John 3:19

miserable and wretched I am! Confounded by the multitude and greatness of my sins, I am compelled to accuse myself.

It was an incredible unkindness, when God spoke to me and called me, that I would not answer Him? What man, so called, would not have heard? Or what man, hearing, would not have answered? If an earthly prince had spoken or called him, I suppose anybody would have willingly done both.

What a wretch and coward I am! When the Prince of Princes, the King of Kings, did speak many pleasant and gentle words to me, and called me so many and various times that they cannot be numbered; and yet, despite these great signs and tokens of love, I would not come to Him. I hid myself out of His sight. I sought and walked so long in many crooked paths that I had totally lost sight of Him.

And it is no marvel or wonder: for I had a blind guide called Ignorance, who dimmed my eyes, that I could never totally get any picture of the fair, good, straight, and right ways of His teaching, but continually followed dangerously in the foul, wicked, crooked, and perverse ways. Yes, and because there were so many following those ways, I could not imagine that I was not walking in the perfect and right way: having more regard for the number of the followers rather than to what they were following. I believed most surely, they were leading me to heaven, whereas I am certain now, they would have brought me down to hell.

I forsook the spiritual honoring of the true, living God, and worshiped visible idols and images made of men's hands,[17] believing that by them I attained heaven. Yes, truly, I made a great idol of myself; for I loved myself better than God. How many things we love or prefer in our hearts before God and receive and esteem them as idols and false gods!

How I have violated this holy, pure, and most high law and commandment concerning loving God, with my whole heart, mind, force, strength, and understanding.[18] And I, as an evil, wicked, disobedient child, gave my will, power, and senses to the contrary, making a god out of almost every earthly and carnal thing.

Furthermore, I did not consider the blood of Christ to be sufficient to wash me from the filth of my sins as He planted in His Word. Rather, I sought such riffraff the Bishop of Rome planted in his tyranny and kingdom. Through the virtue and sacredness of them, I trusted with great confidence to receive full remission of my sins.

And so, I did as much as possible to obscure and darken the great benefit of Christ's passion; and it is not possible to think of anything of greater value. No greater injury and displeasure to almighty God our Father can be done than to tread Christ underfoot, His only-begotten and well-beloved Son. All other sins in the world, gathered together in one, are not as heinous and detestable in the sight of

---

[17] Romans 1:21-28
[18] Luke 10:27

God. And no wonder, for in Christ crucified, God shows Himself to be most noble and glorious, even an almighty God, and most loving Father, in His only dear and chosen blessed Son. And therefore, I count myself one of the most wicked and miserable sinners, because I have been so much against Christ my Savior.

Saint Paul desired to know nothing but Christ crucified,[19] after he had been raptured into the third heaven, where he heard such secrets as were not fitting and proper to speak to men,[20] but counted all his works and doings as nothing, to win Christ[21]. And I, most presumptuously thinking nothing of Christ crucified, went about to set forth my own righteousness,[22] saying with the proud Pharisee:[23] Good Lord, I thank You, I am not like other men; I am no adulterer nor fornicator, and so forth: with such words of vainglory, extolling myself and despising others.

I worked as a hired servant for wages[24] or for reward; and not as a loving child. I should have been working only for the sake of love without respect of wages or reward. Neither did I consider how beneficial a Father I had, who did show me His love and mercy and out of His own simple grace and goodness, when I was most His enemy, He sent His

---

[19] 1 Corinthians 2:2
[20] 2 Corinthians 12:2
[21] Philippians 3:7
[22] Romans 10:3
[23] Luke 18:9-14
[24] John 10:12

only-begotten and well-beloved Son into this world of wretchedness and misery, to suffer most cruel and sharp death for my redemption. But my heart was so stony and hard, that this great benefit was never truly and lively printed in my heart, although I often rehearsed it with my words, thinking myself to be sufficiently instructed in the same, but indeed, being in blind ignorance.

Yet, I stood so well in mine own judgment and opinion, that I thought it vain to seek to increase my knowledge of the work of Christ. Paul calls Christ the wisdom of God, and the same Christ was to me foolishness;[25] my pride and blindness deceived me, and the hardness of my heart opposed the growing of truth within it. Such were the fruits of my carnal and human reason, to receive rotten ignorance instead of valuable ripe and seasonable knowledge. Such also is the malice and wickedness that possesses the hearts of men: the wisdom and pleasing of the flesh.

I professed Christ in my baptism when I began to live but as life continued, I swerved from Him even as an unbaptized heathen. Christ was innocent and void of all sin; and I wallowed in filthy sin, and was free from no sin. Christ was obedient unto His Father, even to the death of the cross;[26] and I disobedient and most stubborn, even to the confusion of truth. Christ was innocent. Christ was meek and humble in heart; and I most proud and

---

[25] 1 Corinthians 1:30
[26] Philippians 2:9

vainglorious. Christ despised the world with all its vanities; and because of the vanities, I made it my God. Christ came to serve His brethren; and I desired to rule over them. Christ despised worldly honor; and I much delighted to attain it. Christ loved the base and simple things of the world; and I esteemed the most fair and pleasant things. Christ loved poverty; and I, wealth. Christ was gentle and merciful to the poor; and I, hardhearted and ungentle. Christ prayed for His enemies; and I hated mine. Christ rejoiced in the conversion of sinners; and I was not grieved to see them return to their sin.

By this declaration, all may understand how far I was from Christ, and without Christ: yes, how contrary to Christ, although I bore the name of a Christian. So much that, if any man had said I had been without Christ, I would have rigidly opposed them. And yet, I neither knew Christ, nor why He came. As concerning the effect and purpose of His coming, I had a certain vain, blind knowledge, both cold and dead, which may be had with all sin: as is plainly true based on this my confession and open declaration.

Why should I now lament, mourn, sigh, and weep for my life, and time spent so evil? With how much humility and lowliness should I come and confess my sins to God, giving Him thanks, that it has pleased Him, out of His abundant goodness, to give me time for repentance?

In considering my sins, I know them to be so grievous, and in number, so exceeding, that I have very often deserved eternal damnation. And, for the deserving of God's wrath, so exceedingly due, I must unceasingly give thanks to the mercy of God, asking also that the same delay of punishment cause not His plague to be more severe, since mine own conscience condemns my former doings.

But His mercy exceeds all iniquity. And, if I should not thus hope: where should I seek refuge and comfort? No mortal man has power to help me; and, for the multitude of my sins, I dare not lift my eyes to heaven where the seat of judgment is. I have so much offended God. What, shall I fall in desperation?

No! I will call upon Christ, the Light of the world, the fountain of life, the relief of all the weary, and the peacemaker between God and man, and the only health and comfort of all true repentant sinners. He can, by His almighty power, save me and deliver me out of this miserable condition. He desires, by His mercy, to save even the entire sin of the world[27]. I have no hope nor confidence in any creature, neither in heaven nor earth, but in Christ, my total and only Savior.

He came into the world to save sinners, and to heal them that are sick; for He said, "The healthy have no need of a physician."[28] Behold, Lord, how I come to You: a sinner, sick and grievously wounded. I am not asking for bread, but for the crumbs that fall from the children's table.[29] Cast me not out of

---

[27] 1 John 2:2
[28] Luke 5:31
[29] Matthew 15:27

Your presence,[30] although I deserve to be cast into hell fire.

If I should look upon my sins, and not upon Your mercy, I should despair. For in myself I find nothing to save me, but a dunghill of wickedness to condemn me. If I should hope, that by mine own strength and power, to come out of this maze of iniquity and wickedness wherein I have walked for so long, I should be deceived. For I am so ignorant, blind, weak, and feeble that I cannot bring myself out of this entangled and wayward maze. The more I seek means and ways to wind myself out of it, the more I am wrapped and entangled in it. So, I perceive my struggling to be a hindrance, and my travail to be labor spent in vain.

It is the hand of the Lord. that can and will bring me out of this endless maze of death; for, without the grace of the Lord that comes before, I cannot ask forgiveness for my sins, nor be repentant or sorry for them. There is no man who can confess that Christ is the only Savior of the world, but by the Holy Spirit: yes, as Saint Paul says, "No man can say 'Jesus Christ is Lord!' but by the Holy Spirit."[31] "The Spirit helps our infirmities, and makes continual intercession for us, with such sorrowful groanings as cannot be expressed."[32]

Therefore, I will first require and pray to the Lord to give me His Holy Spirit: to teach me to confess

---

[30] Psalm 51:11
[31] 1 Corinthians 12:3
[32] Romans 8:26

that Christ is the Savior of the world, and to utter these words, "Jesus Christ is Lord," and finally, to help mine infirmities, and to intercede for me. For I am most certain and sure, that no creature in heaven nor earth is of power, or can by any mean help me, but God, who is omnipotent, almighty, beneficial, and merciful, willing to help, and loving to all those who call, and put their whole confidence and trust in Him. Therefore, I will seek none other means nor advocate, but Christ's Holy Spirit, who is the only Advocate and Mediator between God and man, to help and relieve me.

But, now, what makes me so bold and strong, to presume to come to the Lord with such audacity and boldness, being so great a sinner? Truly, nothing but His own Word: for He says, "Come to me all you that labor, and are burdened, and I shall refresh you."[33] What gentle, merciful, and comfortable words these are to all sinners! What a most gracious, comfortable, and gentle saying, with such pleasant and sweet words to allure His enemies to come to Him! Is there any worldly prince or magistrate that would show such clemency and mercy to their disobedient and rebellious subjects, having offended them? I suppose they would not with such words allure them, unless to entice them whom they cannot capture, and punish them. But even as Christ is Prince of Princes and Lord of Lords, so His charity and mercy surmounts all others.

---

[33] Matthew 11:28

Christ says, "If earthly fathers give good gifts to their children when they ask them, how much more shall your heavenly Father, being in substance holy and gracious, give good gifts to all those who ask Him?"[34] It is no small nor little gift that I require, neither do I think I am worthy to receive such a noble gift, being so ingrate, unkind, and wicked a child. But when I behold the kindliness, liberality, mercy, and goodness of the Lord, I am encouraged, emboldened, and stirred to ask for such a noble gift. The Lord is so bountiful and liberal that He will not allow us to be satisfied and contented with just one gift, nor to ask simple and small gifts.

Therefore, he promises and binds Himself to His Word, to give good and beneficial gifts to all them that ask Him with true faith: without which, nothing can be done acceptable or pleasing to God.[35] For faith is the foundation and ground of all other gifts, virtues, and graces. Therefore, I will say: "Lord, increase my faith."[36] For this is the life everlasting, Lord, that I must believe You to be the true God, and Jesus Christ whom You did send.[37] By this faith I am assured; and by this assurance, I feel the remission of my sins. This makes me bold. This comforts me. This quenches all despair. I know, O my Lord, Your eyes look upon my faith.

---

[34] Matthew 7:11
[35] Hebrews 11:6
[36] Luke 17:5
[37] John 17:3

Saint Paul says we are justified by faith in Christ, and not by the deeds of the law.[38] For if righteousness came by the law, then Christ died in vain.[39] Saint Paul means not a dead, human, historical faith, gotten by human effort, but a supernatural, living faith which works by love, as he himself plainly states.[40]

This esteem of faith does not disparage good works, for out of this faith springs all good works. Yet, we may not impute to the worthiness of faith or good works our justification before God; but ascribe and give the worthiness of it totally to the merits of Christ's passion; and declare and attribute the knowledge and perception of those merits to faith alone. The very true and only property of faith is to take, apprehend, and hold fast the promises of God's mercy, which makes us righteous; and causes me to continually hope for the same mercy; and, in love, to do the many good works ascribed in the Scripture, that I may be thankful for the same.

Thus, I feel myself to come, as it were, in a new garment before God; and now, by His mercy, to be declared just and righteous: which before, without His mercy, was sinful and wicked; and by faith to obtain his mercy, which the unfaithful cannot enjoy. And although Saint John extolls love in his epistle, saying that God is love,[41] and He that dwells in love

---

[38] Romans 3:20
[39] Galatians 2:21
[40] Galatians 5:6
[41] 1 John 4:8

dwells in God:[42] truly, love makes men live like angels; and makes meek lambs out of the most furious, unbridled, and carnal men.

Yes, with how fervent a spirit should I call, cry, and pray to the Lord, to make His great love burn and flame in my heart, being so stony and evil affected, that it never would conceive nor regard the great, inestimable charity and love of God in sending His only-begotten and dear-beloved Son into this vale of misery,[43] to suffer the most cruel and sharp death of the cross for my redemption?

Yet, I never had this unspeakable and abundant love of God properly printed and fixed in my heart until it pleased God, of His simple grace, mercy, and pity, to open my eyes, making me see and behold Christ-crucified to be my only Savior and Redeemer. For then I began (and not before) to perceive and see my own ignorance and blindness because I would not learn to know Christ, my Savior and Redeemer. But when God, of His simple goodness, had thus opened mine eyes,[44] and made me see and behold Christ, the wisdom of God, the Light of the world, through the supernatural eyes of faith: all pleasures, vanities, honor, riches, wealth, and supports of the world began to taste bitter to me.

Then I knew, when such benefits came, that it was no illusion of the devil, nor false nor human doctrine that I had received. What I formerly loved and esteemed, (even though God had forbidden us

---

[42] 1 John 4:16
[43] John 3:16
[44] Ephesians 1:18

to love the world and the vain pleasures and shadows of the world[45]), I now detested. Then I began to understand that Christ was my only Savior and Redeemer, and this same teaching to be completely divine, holy, and heavenly, infused by grace into the hearts of the faithful. This never can be attained by human doctrine nor foolish reason, although they should struggle and work for the same until the end of the world. Then I began to dwell in God by love, knowing that by the loving charity of God, through the remission of my sins, that God is love, as Saint John declares.

I do not take lightly my faith whereby I came to know God, and whereby it pleased God to justify me because I trusted in Him. But many will wonder and marvel at my statement that I never knew Christ as my Savior and Redeemer until this time. For many have this opinion, saying, "Who doesn't know there is a Christ? Who, being a Christian, does not confess Him as his Savior?" And, thus they believe that their dead, human, historical faith and knowledge (which they have learned in their scholastic books) and may be had with all sin (as I said before), to be the true, infused faith and knowledge of Christ. Thus, they say that by their own experience of themselves, that their faith does not justify them. And true it is, except they have this faith, which I have described before, they shall never be justified.

---

[45] 1 John 2:15-17

Yet, it is true that, by faith alone, I am sure to be justified. This being true, many impugn this office and function of true faith because so many lack true faith. As the faithful are compelled to allow true faith, so the unfaithful can in no way claim the same. The one, feeling in himself what he claims to be true; the other, has nothing in himself to claim. I have, certainly, no special learning to completely defend this matter, but a simple zeal and earnest love for the truth, inspired by God, who promises to pour His Spirit upon all flesh: which I have, by the grace of God, whom I most humbly honor, felt in myself to be true.

Part Two

Let us therefore, now, I pray you, by faith, behold and consider the great goodness of God, in sending His Son to suffer death for our redemption when we were His mortal enemies; and after what sort and manner He sent Him.

First it is to be considered, yes, to be undoubtedly believed with a mature faith, that God sent Him to us freely: for He did give Him, and not sell Him. A more noble and rich gift He could not have given. He sent not a servant, or a friend, but His Only Son, so dearly beloved: not in delights, riches, and honors, but in crosses, poverties, and slanders; not as a lord, but as a servant. Yes, in the most vile and painful passions, to wash us: not with water, but with His own precious blood; not from dirt, but from the puddle and filth of our iniquities. He has given Him, not to make us poor, but to enrich us with His divine virtues, merits, and graces:[46] yes, and in Him, He has given us all good things, and, finally, Himself, and with such great love as cannot be expressed.

Was it not a most high and abundant love of God, to send Christ to shed His blood, to lose honor, life, and all, for His enemies? Even at the time when we had done Him the most injury,[47] He first showed His love to us, with such flames of love, that greater could not be shown. God in Christ has opened to us

---

[46] 2 Corinthians 8:9
[47] Romans 5:8

(although we be weak and blind of ourselves) that we may behold, in this miserable state, the great wisdom, goodness, and truth, with all the other godly perfections, which are in Christ.

Therefore, inwardly to behold Christ crucified upon the cross is our best and godliest meditation. We may also see in Christ crucified, the beauty of the soul, better than in all the books of the world. For who, with living faith, sees and feels in spirit that Christ, the Son of God, is dead for the satisfying and the purifying of the soul, shall see that his soul is appointed for the very tabernacle and mansion of the inestimable and incomprehensible majesty and honor of God.

We see also, in Christ crucified, how vain and foolish the world is;[48] and how Christ, being most wise, despised the same. We see also how blind it is; because the world knows not Christ, but persecuted Him. We also see how unkind the world is, by killing Christ, at the time He showed it the most favor. How hard and obstinate was it, that would not be appeased with so many tears, such sweat, and so much bloodshed of the Son of God, suffering with so great and lofty love? Therefore, he is very blind who does not see not how vain, foolish, false, ingrate, cruel, hard, wicked, and evil the world is.

We may also, in Christ crucified, weigh our sins as in a divine balance: how grievous and how weighty they are, seeing they have crucified Christ. They would never have been counterbalanced, but

---

[48] 1 Corinthians 1:20

with the great and precious weight of the blood of the Son of God. And therefore God, of His great goodness, determined that His Blessed Son should rather suffer bloodshed than our sins should have condemned us. We shall never know our own misery and wretchedness, but with the light of Christ crucified. Then, when we feel his mercy, we shall see our own cruelty; when we see his righteousness and holiness, we see our own unrighteousness and iniquity.

Therefore, to learn to know truly our own sins is to study the book of the crucifix[49], by continual discussion in faith. To have perfect and plentiful love is to learn first, by faith, the love that God has towards us. We may see also, in Christ upon the cross, how great the pains of hell and how blessed the joys of heaven are; and what a sharp, painful thing it will be for those who are deprived of that sweet, happy and glorious joy.

Then this crucifix is the book, wherein God has included all things, and has most concisely written therein, all truth profitable and necessary for our salvation. Therefore, let us endeavor ourselves to study this book, that we, being enlightened with the

---

[49] "Book of the Crucifix" is reminiscent of Martin Luther's *Meditation on the Passion of our Lord.* Luther writes: "They contemplate Christ's passion aright who view it with a terror-stricken heart and a despairing conscience. This terror must be felt as you witness the stern wrath and the unchanging earnestness with which God looks upon sin and sinners, so much so that he was unwilling to release sinners even for his only and dearest Son without his payment of the severest penalty for them,"

Spirit of God, may give Him thanks for so great a benefit. If we look further in this book, we shall see Christ's great victory upon the cross: which was so noble and mighty, that there never was, neither shall there ever be such victory.

If the victory and glory of worldly princes were great, because they did overcome great hosts of men, how much more was Christ's greater, which vanquished not only the prince of the world, but all the enemies of God: triumphing over persecution, injuries, villainies, slanders, yes, death, the world, sin, and the devil; and brought to confusion all carnal wisdom.[50]

The princes of the world never fight without the strength of the world. Christ, contrarily, went to war, even against all the strength of the world. He would fight, as David did with Goliath, unarmed of all human wisdom and strategy, and without all worldly power and strength. Nevertheless, He was fully replenished and armed with the whole armor of the Spirit.[51] And in this one battle, he overcame, forever, all His enemies. There was never so glorious a spoil, neither a more rich and noble one, than Christ was upon the cross: which delivered all His elect from such a sharp, miserable captivity. He had, in this battle, many stripes, yes, and lost His life; but His victory was so much greater.

Therefore, when we look upon the Son of God with a supernatural faith and light, so unarmed,

---

[50] Colossians 2:15
[51] Ephesians 6:10

naked, given up, and alone; with humility, patience, liberality, modesty, gentleness, and with the other of His divine virtues; beating down to the ground all God's enemies, and making the soul of man so fair and beautiful: I am forced to say that His victory and triumph was marvelous. And therefore, Christ deserved to have this noble title: "Jesus of Nazareth, King of the Jews."[52]

But if we will specifically unfold and see His great victories, let us first behold how He overcame sin with His innocence, and confounded pride with His humility, quenched all worldly love with His love, appeased the wrath of His Father with His meekness, turned hatred into love with His so many benefits and godly zeal. Christ has not only overcome sin, but rather He has killed the same: since He has made satisfaction for it Himself, with the most holy sacrifice and offering of His precious body, in suffering most bitter and cruel death. Also, He gives to all those who love Him, so much spirit, grace, virtue, and strength, that they may resist, impugn, and overcome sin, and not consent, neither allow it to reign in them.

He has also vanquished sin, because He has taken away the power of sin: that is, He has cancelled the law,[53] which was, in evil men, the occasion of sin. Therefore, sin has no power against them, who are by the Holy Spirit united to Christ; in them there is nothing worthy of damnation. And

---

[52] John 19:21
[53] 1 Corinthians 15:56

although the dregs of Adam do remain, that is, our desires of the flesh, which indeed are sins: nevertheless, they are not imputed as sins, if we are truly joined to Christ.

It is true that Christ might have taken away all our immoderate affections, but He has left them for the greater glory of His Father, and for His own greater triumph. For example: When a prince, fighting with his enemies which had sometime ruled over his people, and subduing them, may kill them if he will, yet he preserves and saves them. And whereas they were lords over his people, he now makes them serve those whom they had ruled. Now, in such a case, the prince does show himself a greater conqueror, in that he has made them to obey, who were rulers; and their subjects who served them, to be lords over them, than if he had utterly destroyed them in the conquest. For, now, he leaves continual victory to those he redeemed: whereas, if the opportunity for victory was taken away, none would remain to be the subjects.

Even so, in like case, Christ has left in us these desires of the flesh, to the intent they should help us to exercise our virtues, where first they did reign over us, to the exercise of our sin. And it may be plainly seen that, whereas first they were such impediments to us, that we could not move ourselves towards God: now by Christ we have so much strength that, notwithstanding the force of them, we may assuredly walk to heaven. And although the children of God sometime do fall by frailty into some sin, yet that falling causes them to humble themselves, and to acknowledge the goodness of God, and to come to Him for refuge and help.[54]

Likewise, Christ, with His death, has overcome the prince of devils with all his host, and has destroyed them all. For, as Paul says: This is verified, that Christ should break the serpent's head, prophesied by God. Although the devil tempts us, yet if by faith we are joined to Christ, we shall not perish; but rather, by his temptation, take great force and might. So, it is evident that the triumph, victory, and glory of Christ is the greater, having subdued the devil that, whereas he was prince and lord of the world, holding all creatures in captivity, now Christ uses him as an instrument to punish the wicked, and to exercise and strengthen the elect of God in Christian warfare.[55]

Christ likewise has overcome death in a more glorious manner (if it be possible), because He has not taken it away, but leaving universally all subject to the same fate. He has given so much virtue and spirit that, whereas before we passed through death with great fear, now we are bold, through the Spirit, for the sure hope of resurrection, that we receive it with joy. It is now no more bitter, but sweet; no more feared, but desired. It is not death, but life.[56]

And, also, it has pleased God that the infirmities and adversities do remain in the sight of the world;

---

[54] Romans 7
[55] 1 John 3:8
[56] 1 Corinthians 15:56

but the children of God are, by Christ, made so strong, righteous, whole and sound, that the troubles of the world are comforts of the spirit; the passions of the flesh are medicines of the soul. For all manner of things work to their service and good;[57] for they in spirit feel that God, their Father, doth govern them, and arranges all things for their benefit; therefore, they feel themselves secure. In persecution, they are quiet and peaceful; in time of trouble, they are without weariness, fears, anxieties, suspicions, miseries; and finally, all the good and evil of the world works to their service.

Moreover, they see that the triumph of Christ has been so great, that not only has He subdued and vanquished all our enemies and the power of them, but He has overthrown and vanquished them in such a manner that all things serve to our well-being. He might and could have taken them all away, but where, then, should have been our victory, palm, and crown? For we daily have struggles in the flesh, and, by the support of grace, have continual victories over sin, giving us cause to glorify God that, by His Son, He has weakened our enemy the devil and, by His Spirit, gives us strength to vanquish his offspring.[58]

So, we acknowledge daily the great triumph of our Savior, and rejoice in our own wonders, which we can in no way impute to any wisdom of this world whereby sin increases. And where worldly wisdom

---

[57] Roman 8:28
[58] Romans 8:38-39

governs most, there sin rules most. For as the world is the enemy of God, so also the wisdom of the world is against God. Christ has declared and exposed the wisdom of the world as foolishness.[59] And although He could have taken away all worldly wisdom, yet He has left it for His greater glory, and triumph of His chosen vessels.

For before, the world was our ruler against God, now, by Christ, we are served by it for God. While still a slave in worldly things; this is not the case when considering supernatural things. If any time men would oppose and contradict us with the wisdom of the world, yet we have, in Christ, so much supernatural light of the truth, that we make a mockery of all those who oppose the truth.

Christ, also, upon the cross, has triumphed over the world. First, because He has discovered the world to be nothing: that whereas it was covered by the veil of hypocrisy and the garment of moral virtues, Christ has showed that, in God's sight, the righteousness of the world is wickedness; and He has borne witness that the works of men, not regenerated by Him in faith, are evil. And so, Christ has judged and condemned the world as nothing.

Furthermore, He has given to all His, so much light and spirit, that they know it, and disapprove the same: yes, and tread it under their feet, with all vain honors, dignities, and pleasures, not accepting the fair promises, nor the offers it presents. No, they

---

[59] 1 Corinthians 3:19

rather scorn them. And, as for the threats and might of the world, they have nothing to fear.

Now, therefore, we may see how great the victory and triumph of Christ is, who has delivered all those the Father gave Him from the power of the devil, cancelling, upon the cross, the writing of our debts.[60] For He has delivered us from the condemnation of sin, from the bondage of the law, from the fear of death, from the danger of the world, and from all evils in this life, and in the world to come.

And He has enriched us, made us noble and most highly happy, so tongues cannot express such a glorious and triumphant way. Therefore, we are forced to say: "His triumph is marvelous!"

It is also seen and known that Christ is the true Messiah, for He has delivered man from all evils; and through Him, man has all goodness, so that He is the true Messiah. Therefore, all other helpers are vain and counterfeit saviors, seeing that, by this our Messiah, Christ, completely and only, we are delivered from all evils and, in Him, we have all goodness.

It is evident and clear that this is true, because the true Christian is a Christian by Christ. And the true Christian senses inwardly, through Christ, so much goodness of God, that even troublesome life and death are sweet to him, and miseries, happy. The true Christian, through Christ, is unburdened: from the servitude of the law, having the law of grace

---

[60] Colossians 2:14

(graven by the Spirit) inhabiting his heart, and from sin that reigned in him, from the power of the demonic spirits, from damnation, and from every evil; and is made a son of God, a brother of Christ, heir of heaven, and lord of the world. So that in Christ, and through Christ, he possesses all good things.

And know that Christ still fights in spirit in His elect vessels, and shall fight even to the day of judgment. At which day shall the great enemy, death, be wholly destroyed,[61] and shall be no more. Then shall the children of God rejoice in Him, saying: "O death, where is thy victory and sting?"[62] There shall be, then, no more trouble nor sin, no evil: but heaven for the good, and hell for the wicked. Then the victory of triumph of Christ shall be fully discovered: who (according to Paul) shall present to His Father the kingdom, together with His chosen, saved by Him.[63] It was no little favor towards His children, that Christ was chosen of God to save us, His elect, so exceedingly, by the way of the cross. Paul calls it a grace, and a most singular grace.

We may well think that He, having been to the world so valiant a captain of God, was full of light, grace, virtue, and spirit. Therefore, He might justly say: "It is finished!" We, seeing then that the triumph and victory of our captain Christ is so marvelous, glorious, and noble and to the battle we

---

[61] 1 Corinthians 15:56
[62] 1 Corinthians 15:55
[63] 1 Corinthians 15:24

are appointed: let us force ourselves to follow Him, by bearing our cross, that we may have fellowship with Him in His kingdom.

It is most justly true that to behold Christ crucified, in spirit, is the best meditation that can be. I certainly never knew my own miseries and contentions so well, by reading books, receiving admonition, or correction, as I have done by considering the spiritual book of the crucifix. I greatly lament that I have passed so many years not regarding that divine book, but I judged and thought myself to be well instructed in the same: whereas now I am of this opinion, that if God would allow me to live here for thousand years, and I should study continually in the same divine book, I would not complete the contemplation of it.

Nor am I contented, but always have a great desire to learn and study more. I never knew my own wickedness, neither truly lamented for my sins until the time that God inspired me with His grace, that I looked in this book of the crucifix. Then I began to see perfectly, that my own power and strength could not help me, and that I was in the Lord's hand: even as the clay is in the potter's hand. Then I began to cry, and say: "Alas, Lord, I have so wickedly offended You, and You have been to me from the beginning so gracious and so good a Father, and most especially, now you have declared and showed Your goodness to me when, in the time I have done You the most injury, to call me, and to make me to know and take You for my Savior and Redeemer."

Such are the wonderful works of God, to call sinners to repentance, and to have them receive Christ, His well-beloved Son, as their Savior. This is the gift of God for all Christians to require and desire. For, unless this great benefit of Christ crucified is felt and fixed surely in man's heart, there can be no good work done, acceptable before God. For in Christ is all fullness of the Godhead[64] and in Him are hid all the treasures of wisdom and knowledge.[65] He is the water of life, whereof whosoever shall drink, shall never thirst; but it shall be in him a well of water, springing up into everlasting life.[66] Saint Paul says there is no condemnation to them who are in Christ, who walk not after the flesh, but after the spirit.[67] Moreover, he says: "If when we were enemies, we were reconciled to God by the death of His Son, how much more, being reconciled, we shall be preserved by His death."[68] It is no little or small benefit we have received by Christ, if we consider what He has done for us, as I have now perfectly declared.

Wherefore, I pray the Lord that this great benefit of Christ crucified may be steadfastly fixed and printed in all Christian hearts, that they may be true lovers of God, and work as children, for love, and not as servants, compelled with threats or incited with hire. The sincere and pure lovers of God do

---

[64] Colossians 2:9
[65] Colossians 2:3
[66] John 4:14
[67] Romans 8:1
[68] Romans 5:10

embrace Christ with such fervency of spirit, that they rejoice in hope, are bold in danger, suffer in adversity, continue in prayer, bless their persecutors; further, they are not wise in their own opinion, neither high-minded in their prosperity, neither ashamed in their adversity, but humble and gentle, always, to all men. For they know that by their faith they are all members of one body, and they have possessed all, one God, one faith, one baptism, one joy, and one salvation.

Part Three

If these pure and sincere lovers of God were abundantly sown, there would not be so much contention and strife growing in the fields of our religion, as there is. Well, I shall pray to the Lord to take all contention and strife away, and that the sowers of sedition may have mind to cease their labor, or to sow it among the stones; and to have grace to sow gracious virtues, where they may both root and bring forth fruit, sending a godly unity and concord among all Christians, that we may serve the Lord in true holiness of life.

The example of good living is required of all Christians, but especially for the ecclesiastical pastors, and shepherds: for they are called in Scripture, workers with God, disbursers of God's mysteries, the light of the world, the salt of the earth, at whose hands all others should take comfort, in the working knowledge of God's will, and purpose, to become children of the light, and taste of appropriate wisdom. They have, or should have, the Holy Spirit abundantly, to pronounce and set forth the Word of God, in clarity and truth. If ignorance and blindness reign among us, they should, with the truth of God's Word, instruct and set before us the truth, and direct us in the way of the Lord.

But thank the Lord, who has now sent us such a godly and learned King, in these latter days, to reign over us: that, with the virtue and force of God's Word, he has taken away the veils and mists of errors, and brought us to the knowledge of the truth by the light of God's Word, which was so long hidden and kept suppressed, that the people were nearly famished and hungered for lack of spiritual food. Such was the charity of the spiritual clergy, and shepherds. But our Moses, and most godly, wise governor and King, has delivered us out of the captivity and bondage of Pharaoh.

By Moses, I mean King Henry the eighth, my most sovereign, favorable lord and husband: who, through the excellent grace of God, is suitable to be an expressed picture of Moses' conquest over Pharaoh. And by Pharaoh, I mean the Bishop of Rome, who has been and is a greater persecutor of all true Christians than ever was Pharaoh of the children of Israel.[69]

For he is a persecutor of the Gospel and grace, a promoter of all superstition and counterfeit holiness, bringing many souls to hell with his alchemy[70] and counterfeit money, deceiving the poor souls under the pretense of holiness; but so much the greater shall be his damnation, because he deceives and robs under Christ's mantle.

The Lord keep and defend all men from his juggling and craftiness, but specially the poor, simple, unlearned souls. And this lesson I wish all men had of him, that when they begin to dislike his

---

[69] It is evident that Katherine wrote this while King Henry was still alive even though it was published after his death.

[70] Possible reference to transubstantiation.

doing, only then they begin to like God, and certainly not before.

As for the spiritual pastors, and shepherds, I think they will cling and hold fast to the Word of God, even to death, to vanquish all God's enemies. If need requires, to lay aside all respects of honor, dignity, riches, wealth, and their private possessions, following also the examples of Christ and His chosen apostles, in preaching and teaching sincere, pure, and wholesome doctrine, and such things as make for peace, with godly lessons, wherewith they may edify others: that every man may walk after his vocation, in holiness of life, in unity and concord. Such unity is to be desired for all true Christians.

It is much to be lamented: the schisms, diversities, contentions, and disputations that have been, and are, in the world about the Christian religion. There is no agreement or unity among the learned men. Truly, the devil has been the sower of sedition, and shall be the maintainer of it, even till God's will is fulfilled. There is no war so cruel and evil as this: for the war with swords kills only the bodies, but this war destroys many souls.

For the poor, unlearned people remain confused, and almost everyone believes and goes his own way, and yet there is but one truth of God's Word, by which we shall be saved. Happy are they who receive it; and most unhappy are they who neglect and persecute it. For it shall be easier for Sodom and Gomorrah at the day of judgment, than for them. And not without just cause, if we consider the benevolence, goodness, and mercy of God: who hath declared His love toward us, greater and more laudable, than He ever did to the Hebrews. For they lived under shadows and figures, and were bound to the law. And Christ has delivered us from the bondage of the law, and has fulfilled all that was prefigured in their law, and in their prophets: shedding His own precious blood to make us the children of His Father, and His brethren. He has made us free, setting us in a godly liberty. Of course, I do not mean license to sin, as many gladly interpret when the subject of Christian liberty is discussed.

Truly, it is not a good spirit that causes men to find fault with everything; and when issues are properly presented, to pervert them into an evil sense and meaning. There are in the world many speakers of holiness and good works; but very rarely and seldom is it declared what those good and holy works are. The fruit of the Spirit is almost never spoken of. Therefore, very few know what they are.

I am truly able to justify the great ignorance of the people: not in this matter alone, but in many others, which are very necessary for Christians to know, because I have much evidence of this. It causes me great sorrow and grief in my heart to speak of such a miserable ignorance and blindness among the people. Certainly, we all can say, "Lord, Lord."[71] But I fear that God may say to us: "This people honors me with their lips, but their hearts

---

[71] Matthew 7:21

are far from me."[72] God desires nothing but the heart, and says that He will be worshipped in spirit and in truth.[73] Christ condemned all hypocrisy and false holiness, and taught sincere, pure, and true godliness. But we, worse than demented or blind, will not follow Christ's doctrine, but trust in men's doctrines, judgments, and sayings, which dim our eyes: and so, the blind leads the blind, and both fall into the ditch.[74]

Truly, in my simple and unlearned judgment, no man's doctrine is to be esteemed, or preferred to Christ's and the Apostles', nor to be taught as a perfect and true doctrine, but only as it does agree with the doctrine of the Gospel. Those who are called spiritual pastors, even though they are most carnal as is evident and clear by their fruits, are so blinded with the love of themselves and the world, that they extol men's inventions and doctrines before the doctrine of the Gospel.

And when they are not able to maintain their own inventions and doctrine with any jot of the Scripture, they cruelly persecute those who don't agree with them. Are such the lovers of Christ? No! No! They are the lovers of wicked Mammon, neither regarding God nor His honor. For filthy lucre[75] has undoubtedly made them nearly mad. This miserable state of spiritual men in the world is to be greatly lamented by all sincere Christians.

---

[72] Matthew 15:8
[73] John 4:4
[74] Matthew 15:14
[75] Titus 1:11: Money

Yet, I cannot permit nor praise all kinds of complaints, but such as may stand with Christian love. Love suffers long, and is gentle; does not envy, chastises no man, does not throw man's faults in his teeth, but refers all things to God:[76] being angry without sin[77], reforming others without slanders, ever bearing a storehouse of mild words to pierce the stonyhearted.

I wish all Christians, that as they have professed Christ, would so endeavor to follow Him in godly living. For we have not put on Christ to live any more to ourselves, in the vanities, delights, and pleasures of the world and the flesh, permitting the desires and carnality of the flesh to have full sway. For we must walk after the Spirit, and not after the flesh. For the Spirit is spiritual, and desires spiritual things, and the flesh carnal, and desires carnal things.[78] Those regenerate in Christ despise the world, and all the vanities and pleasures of the world.[79]

They are not lovers of themselves, for they feel how evil and weak they are, not able to do any good thing without the help of God, from whom they acknowledge all good things to proceed. They do not flatter themselves and think that everything that shines in the world is good and holy, for they know that all external and outward works that are not so

---

[76] 1 Corinthians 13
[77] Ephesians 4:26
[78] Galatians 5:17
[79] 1 John 2:15-17

glorious and fair to the world, may still be prompted by evil as well as of good. Therefore, they have very little estimate for the outward show of holiness, because they are spiritual, casting their eyes upon heavenly things and neither looking nor regarding the earthly things for they are to them vile and dismal.[80]

They have also the simplicity of the dove, and the strategy of the serpent.[81] They simply have a desire to do good to all men and to hurt no man, even though they may have opportunity. And in practice, they neither give nor minister any reason for any man to rebuke their doctrine. They also are not as a reed shaken with every wind.[82] When they are blasted with tempests and storms of the world, they remain firm, stable, and quiet, feeling in spirit that God, as their best Father, does send and allow all things for their benefit and service. Christ is to them a rule, a line, an example of the Christian life. They are never offended at anything, although occasion arises.

For like as Christ, when Peter tried to dissuade Him from going to his death, answered and said, "Go back from me, Satan,[83] for you are offensive. As much as possible, you give me occasion with your words to make me withdraw myself from death, although I do not yield. For you cannot extinguish

---

[80] Romans 8:5-8
[81] Matthew 10:17
[82] Matthew 11:17
[83] Matthew 16:23

the burning desire I have to shed My blood for My chosen."

Even so, the mature Christians are never offended at anything. For although the world was full of sin, they would not withdraw themselves from doing good, nor wax cold in the love of the Lord. And much less would they be moved to be evil; yes, rather they are so much more moved to do good.

The regenerated by Christ are never offended at the works of God, because they know by faith that God does all things well, and that He cannot err, neither for lack of power, nor by ignorance, nor malice. For they know Him to be almighty, and that He sees all things, and is most abundantly good. They see and feel in spirit that out of the highest perfect will, cannot but proceed most perfect works.

Likewise, they are not offended by the works of men: for, if those works are good, they are moved by them to take opportunity to follow them, and to acknowledge the goodness of God, while giving thanks and daily praising His name. But if the works of men are indifferent, and may be done with either good or evil intention, they judge the best part, thinking they may be done for a good purpose, and so, they are edified. But if those works of men are so evil that they cannot in any way be taken as good, yet they are not offended, although they very well could be. No, rather they are edified, using the occasion to bear fruit, although the opposite is presented to them. Then they begin to think and say: "If God had not preserved me with His grace, I should have committed this sin, and worse. O how much am I bound to confess and acknowledge the goodness of God!"

They also further think and say: "He that has sinned may be one of God's elect; perhaps the Lord has allowed him to fall so that he may know himself better. I know he is one of them for whom Christ has shed His blood, and one of my Christian brethren. Truly I will admonish and rebuke him; and in case I find him desperate, I will comfort him and show him the great goodness and mercy of God, in Christ; and with godly consolations I will see if I can lift him up again." So, you see how those regenerated by Christ, in all matters win and receive fruits.

On the other hand, the ignorant and immature are offended at small trivialities, judging everything to be evil, grudging and murmuring against their neighbor; and, in addition, they demonstrate such fervency so that they judged by the blind world as being great zeal-bearers for God.

But this is not the greatest evil of the ignorant. I fear they are so blind and ignorant that they are also offended by good things, and judge nothing good but that which they accept and esteem to be good, murmuring against all who do not follow their ways.

If there are any like this, I pray that the Lord give them the light of His truth, that they may increase and grow in godly strength. I suppose if such ignorant and immature had seen Christ and His disciples eat meat with unwashed hands,[84] or not to have fasted with the Pharisees, they would have

---

[84] Mark 7:2

been offended, seeing Him a breaker of men's traditions. While their desires incline their eyes to see through other men, they see nothing in themselves. Love, on the other hand considers no one evil, but discreetly and properly interprets all actions, taking everything justly and honestly.

Now these superstitious weaklings, if they had known Christ, and saw the way he led His life, sometimes with women, sometimes with Samaritans, with publicans, sinners, and with the Pharisees, they would have murmured against Him. Also, if they had seen Mary pour the precious ointment on Christ, they would have said with Judas: "This ointment could have been sold, and given to the poor."[85] If they also had seen Christ with whips[86] drive out of the Temple those who bought and sold, they would have immediately judged Christ to have been anxious and moved with anger, and not by zealous love. How they would have been offended, if they had seen Him going to the Jews' feast, heal a sick man on the Sabbath day,[87] converse with the woman of Samaria,[88] yes, and show her His most divine teaching and life. They would have taken the opportunity to hate and persecute Him, as did the scribes and Pharisees. Christ, the Savior of the world, would have been offensive and destructive to them.

---

[85] John 12:5
[86] John 2:15
[87] Mark 3:1-6
[88] John 4

There is another type of the ignorant and immature who are offended in this manner: when they see someone who is considered and esteemed to be holy, commit sin, immediately they learn to do the same, and worse. They grow cold in doing good, and confirm themselves in evil.

And then they excuse their wicked life by revealing the sin of their neighbor and thereby slander him. If any man corrects them, they say: "Such a man did this, and worse." So, it is evident that such individuals would deny Christ, if they saw others do the same.

If they went to Rome and saw the abominations of the priests, which is reported to reign among them, and they saw one sin who was reputed and assumed to be holy, their faith would be lost: but not the true faith in Christ which they never possessed. But they would lose the human opinion they had of the goodness of the priests. For if they had faith in Christ, the Holy Spirit, who would be mighty in them, would witness to them, that in case all the world would deny Christ, they would remain firm and stable in the true faith.

The Pharisees also took opportunity by the evil of others to grow haughty and proud, taking themselves to be men of greater perfection than any other because of their virtue, as they did when they saw the publican's confession. And so, they are offended with every little thing, judging evil, murmuring against their neighbor; and, for that reason, they are reputed by many as being more holy and good, but, indeed, they are more wicked.

The most wicked persons are offended even at themselves; for at their little stability in goodness, and of their detestable and evil life, they take occasion to despair. They should instead commit themselves more to God, asking mercy for their offenses, and immediately giving thanks, that it hath pleased God, out of His goodness, to put up with them for such a long a time.

But, what more can be said? The evil men are even offended at the works Of God. They see God put up with sinners. Therefore, they think that sin does not displease Him. And because they see that the good are not rewarded with riches, they often imagine that God does not love them. It seems to them God is partial, because He hath elected some, and some reproved. They use that as an occasion to do evil saying, "Whatsoever God hath determined, shall take place"

If they also see the good men oppressed, and the evil men exalted, they judge God unjust, taking occasion to do evil, saying: "Since God favors the evil men, let us do evil enough, so that He does us good." If, then, the wicked be offended even at God, it is no wonder if they are offended by those who follow and walk in His paths and ways.

Now I will speak, with great sadness and heaviness in my heart, of a sort of people who are in the world, that are called "professors of the Gospel" and by their words declare and show, they are deeply affected by the same. But, I am afraid, some of them have built upon the sand, as Simon Magus[89] did, making a weak foundation. I mean, they don't make Christ their chief foundation, professing His doctrine out of a sincere, pure, and zealous mind. Either, because they are called "gospellers," they seek to gain some credit and good opinions from the sincere and appreciative of Christ's doctrine, or to find out some fleshly liberty, or to be contentious disputers, finders, or rebukers of other men's faults, or else, finally, to please and flatter the world. Such "gospellers" are an offense and a slander to the Word of God, and make the wicked rejoice and laugh at them, saying: "Behold, I pray you, their fair fruits. What love, what discretion, what godliness, holiness, or purity of life is amongst them? Be they not great avengers, foul gluttons, slanderers, backbiters, adulterers, fornicators, swearers, and blasphemers?"

Yes, they stagger and tumble in all these sins; these are the fruits of their doctrine. And thus, it is seen how the Word of God is spoken of as evil, through licentious and evil living.

And yet the Word of God is all holy, pure, sincere, and godly, being the teaching and motivation for all holy and pure living. It is the wicked who pervert all good things into evil, for an evil tree cannot bring forth good fruit. And when good seed is sown in a barren and evil ground, it yields no good crop, and so it is with the Word of God. For when it is heard and known of wicked men, it brings forth no good

---

[89] Acts 8:9-24

fruit; but when it is sown in good ground, I mean the hearts of good people, it brings forth good fruit abundantly:[90] so that the lack and fault is in men, and not in the Word of God.

I pray God that all men and women may have grace to become good ground for the fruits of the Gospel, and to only forsake all the wrangling over it. For only speaking of the Gospel does not make men good Christians, but merely good talkers, unless their facts and works agree with the same. Their speech is good, because their hearts are good.[91]

So much talk of the Word of God, without practicing the same in our living, is evil and detestable in the sight of God. It is lamentable to hear that there are many in the world who do not properly digest the reading of Scripture, and commend and praise ignorance, and say that much knowledge of God's Word is the origin of all dissension, schisms, and contention, and makes men haughty, proud, and presumptuous by reading of the same.

This manner of saying is no less than a plain blasphemy against the Holy Spirit. For the Spirit of God is the author of His Word, and so the Holy Spirit is made the author of evil: which is the greatest blasphemy and, as the Scripture says, a sin that shall not be forgiven in this world, neither in the one to come.[92]

---

[90] Matthew 13:3-9
[91] Luke 6:45
[92] Matthew 21:31-32

All of us have the duty, to procure and seek all the ways and means possible, to have more knowledge of God's Word set forth abroad in this world, and to not allow ignorance, and opposition to the knowledge of God's Word to stop the mouths of the unlearned with subtle and crafty persuasions of philosophy and sophistry. This produces no fruit, but a great distress to the minds of the simple and ignorant because they will not know which way to turn.

It is an extreme wickedness to charge the holy, sanctified Word of God with the offenses of men, to allege the Scriptures to be perilous learning because certain readers fall into heresies. These men might be forced, by this kind of argument, to forsake the use of fire because fire burned their neighbor's house, or to abstain from meat or drink because they see many gluttons. O blind hate! They slander God for man's offense, and excuse the man who offends, and blame the Scripture, which they cannot improve.

Yes, I have heard of some who very well understood the Latin language who, when they have heard educated men persuade concerning the credit and belief of certain "unwritten verities"[93] as they call them, which are not expressed in Scripture, and are yet taught as apostolic doctrine and necessary to be believed. They contend that educated men

---

[93] When the Bible became available in English, it became evident that there were many doctrines taught by Rome that were not found in Scripture. These became known as "unwritten truths" that were only known to the educated clergy.

have more "epistles" written by the apostles of Christ than we have in the canon of the Old and New Testament. These unwritten verities are only known by the clergy.

I was greatly grieved to hear this and think that any person could have such a blind, ignorant opinion. Some simple explanations are to be praised, but this simplicity, devoid of truth, I can neither praise nor condone. And thus, it may be seen how we who are unlettered remain confused, without God and His grace to lighten our hearts and minds with a heavenly light and knowledge of His will. For of ourselves, we are given to believe men more than God. I pray that God would send the Spirit of God abundantly to all learned men, that their doctrine may bring forth the fruits thereof.

I suppose there was never a greater need for good doctrine to be set forth in the world than in this age: for the carnal children of Adam are so wise in their generation that, if it were possible, they would deceive the children of light. The world loves his own, and therefore their facts and works are highly esteemed by the world. But the children of God are hated because they are not of the world. For their habitation is in heaven, and they despise the world as a most vile slave.

The fleshly children of Adam are so political, subtle, crafty, and wise in their kind that the elect should be deluded, if it were possible. For in outer appearance, they are clothed with Christ's garment with a fair show of all godliness and holiness in their words. But they have so shorn, trimmed, and twisted Christ's garment and so disguised themselves, that the children of light, beholding them with a spiritual eye, account and take them for mere men who have sold their Master's garment, and have stolen a piece of every man's garment.

Yet, by their subtle art and crafty wits, they have so put those patches and pieces together that they make the blind world and carnal men believe it is Christ's very mantle. But the children of light know better. For they are led by the Spirit of God to the knowledge of the truth; and therefore, they discern and judge all things properly, and know from where they come: even from the bishop of Rome and his members, the chief source of all pride, vainglory, ambition, hypocrisy, and false holiness.

The children of God are not ashamed, although the world hate them. They believe they are in the grace and favor of God, and that He, as a best Father, does govern them in all things, putting away from them all vain confidence, and trust in their own doings. For they know, by themselves, they can do nothing but sin. They are not so foolish and childish, not to give God thanks for their election, which was before the beginning of the world.[94] For they believe most surely, they are of the chosen: for the Holy Spirit does witness to their spirit that they are the children of God, and therefore they believe God rather than man.[95] They say with Saint Paul: "Who shall separate us from the love of God? Shall

---

[94] Ephesians 1:4
[95] Romans 8:16

tribulation, anguish, persecution, hunger, nakedness, peril, or sword? As it is written: For Your sake, we are killed all day long, and are counted as sheep appointed to be slain. Nevertheless, in all these things, we overcome through Him that loveth us. For I am sure that neither death, nor life, nor angels, nor rule, neither power, neither things present, neither things to come, neither quantity or quality, neither any creature, shall be able to depart us from the love of God, which is in Christ Jesus our Lord."[96]

They are not arrogantly inflamed by this godly faith, nor do they become loose, idle, or slow in doing godly works, rather, they are so much more fervent in doing most holy and pure works, which God has commanded them to walk in.[97] They wander not in men's traditions and inventions, leaving the most holy and pure precepts of God undone, which they know they are bound to observe and keep.

Also, they work not like hirelings for wages, or reward, but as loving children, without respect of money, gain, or position. They are in such liberty of spirit, and joy so much in God, that their inward consolation cannot be expressed with tongue. All fear of damnation is gone from them, for they have put their whole hope of salvation in His hands, who will and can perform it. Neither have they any post or pillar to lean upon, but God and His smooth and

---

[96] Romans 8:38-39
[97] Ephesians 2:10

unwrinkled Church.[98] For He is to them All in all things, and to Him they lean, as a most sure, square pillar, in prosperity and adversity, not doubting His promises and covenants, for they believe most certainly they shall be fulfilled.

Also, the children of God are not curious in searching the high mysteries of God, which are not proper for them to know. Neither do they go about with human and carnal reasons to interpret Scripture, persuading men, by their subtle wits and carnal doctrine, that much knowledge of Scripture makes men heretics, unless they dilute it with human doctrine, philosophy, and logic: and thus, be seduced according to the traditions of men, after the ordinances of the world, and not after Christ. Saint Paul does most diligently admonish us, which arts are not convenient and proper to rival Scripture.[99] For the Scriptures are so pure and holy that no perfection can be added to them. For even as fine gold doth excel all other metals, so doth the Word of God excel over all men's doctrines.

I ask the Lord to send the learned and unlearned such abundance of His Holy Spirit, that they may obey and observe the most sincere and holy Word of God. And show the fruits thereof, which consists chiefly in love and godly unity: that, as we have professed one God, one faith, and one baptism,[100] so we may be all of one mind and one accord, putting

---

[98] Ephesians 5:27
[99] Colossians 2:8
[100] Ephesians 4:5

away all biting and gnawing; for, in backbiting, slandering, and misrepresenting our Christian brethren, we do not show ourselves to be the disciples of Christ, whom we profess.[101]

In Him was extraordinary love, humility, and patience, suffering most patiently all ignominy, rebukes, and slanders, praying to His Eternal Father for His enemies with most fervent love: and in all things, when He prayed on the Mount, did submit His will to His Father's.[102] A goodly example and lesson for us to follow in all times and seasons, as well as in prosperity as in adversity: to have no will but God's will, committing and leaving to Him all our cares and griefs, and to abandon all our strategies and inventions, for they are most vain and foolish, and, indeed, very shadows and daydreams.

But we are yet so carnal and fleshly that we come headlong, like unbridled colts, without bridle or bit. If we had the love of God printed in our hearts, it would hinder us from running astray. And until it please God to send us this bit to hold us in, we will never run in the right direction, although we may never speak and talk so much of God and His Word.

The true followers of Christ's teaching always have a respect and an eye to their vocation.

If they are called to the ministry of God's Word, they preach and teach it sincerely, to the edifying of others, and show themselves, in their living, followers of the same. If they are married men,

---

[101] 1 Peter 2:1
[102] Luke 22:42

having children and family, they nourish and bring them up, without bitterness and harshness, in the doctrine of the Lord; in all godliness and virtue, They commit the instruction of others, who are not under their care, to the improvement of God and His ministers, who are chiefly kings and princes, bearing the sword even for that purpose, to punish evildoers.

If they are children, they honor their father and mother, knowing it to be God's commandment, and that He has thereto attached a promise of long life.

If they are servants, they obey and serve their masters with all fear and reverence, even for the Lord's sake, neither with murmuring nor grudging, but with a free heart and mind.

If they are husbands, they love their wives as their own bodies, after the example as Christ loved the church, and gave Himself for it, to make it to Him a bride, without spot or wrinkle.[103]

If they are married women, they learn of Saint Paul, to be obedient to their husbands, and to keep silence in the congregation, and to learn from their husbands, at home.[104] Also, they wear such apparel as befits holiness and suitable usage, with soberness: not being accusers or detractors, not given too much to the eating of delicacies and drinking of wine. But they teach honest things, to make the young women sober-minded, to love their husbands, to love their children, to be discreet,

---

[103] Ephesians 5:25-26
[104] 1 Corinthians 14:34

81

chaste, domesticated, good, obedient unto their husbands, that the Word of God be not evil spoken of.

Truly, if all sorts of people would look to their own vocation, and order the same according to Christ's teaching, we should not have so many eyes and ears beholding other men's faults as we have. For we are so busy and glad to find and spy out other men's doings, that we forget and have no time to weigh and ponder our own: which we ought to first reform after the Word of God, and then we shall be better at helping another with the straw in his eyes.[105]

But, alas, we are so much given to love and to flatter ourselves, and so blinded with carnal affections, that we can see and perceive no fault in ourselves. And therefore, it is required and necessary for us, to pray with one heart and mind to God, to give us a heavenly light and knowledge of our own miseries and calamities, that we may truly see them and acknowledge them before Him.

If any man shall be offended at this my lamenting the faults of men which are in the world, imagining that I do it either out of hatred or spite to any sort or kind of people: truly, in so doing, they do me a great wrong. For I thank God, by His grace, I hate no person; yes, I would say more, to give witness to my conscience, that neither life, honor, riches, nor whatsoever I possess here, which pertains to my own private possessions, be it never

---

[105] Matthew 7:3

so dearly loved by me, that most willingly and gladly I would leave it, to win any man to Christ, of whatever degree or sort he was.

And yet this is nothing in comparison to the love that God hath shown me, in sending Christ to die for me: no, if I had all the love of angels and apostles, it should be but like a spark of fire compared to a great heap of burning coals. God knows my intentions and mind. I have lamented my own sins and faults to the world. I trust nobody will judge I have done it for praise or the thanks of any person, since rather I might be ashamed than rejoice in rehearsing them. For if they know how little I esteem and weigh the praise of the world, that opinion would soon be removed and taken away.

For I thank God, that by His grace, I know the world to be a blind judge, and the praises thereof vain and of little consequence, and therefore I seek not the praises of the same, neither to satisfy it in no other way than I am taught by Christ to do, according to Christian love.

I would to God we would all, when occasion arises, confess our faults to the world, laying aside all respect to our own position. But, alas, self-love so reigns among us that, as I have said before, we cannot spy our own faults. And if perhaps we should discover our own guilt, we either favorably interpret it as not being sin, or else we are ashamed to confess it. Yes, and we are badly offended and grieved to hear another tell us our faults in a lovingly and godly manner, making no distinction between a loving warning and malicious accusation.

Truly, if we sought God's glory, as we should do in all things, we should not be ashamed to confess ourselves as deviating from God's commands and ordinances, when it is obvious that we have done so, and, in fact, daily do.

I pray God our own faults and deeds condemn us not, at the last day, when every man shall be rewarded according to his doings. Truly, if we do not redress and amend our living, according to the teaching of the Gospel, we shall receive a terrible sentence by Christ, the Son of God, when He shall come to judge and condemn all transgressors and breakers of His precepts and commandments, and to reward all His obedient and loving children.

We shall have no lawyer to make a plea for us, neither can we have the day delayed; neither will the just Judge be corrupted with affection, bribes, or reward; neither will He hear any excuse or delay; neither shall this saint or that martyr help us, be they ever so holy; neither shall our ignorance save us from damnation. But, yet, willful blindness and obstinate ignorance shall receive greater punishment, and not without just cause. Then shall it be known who has walked in the dark, for all things shall appear manifest before him. No man's deeds shall be hidden, no, neither words nor thoughts.

The poor and simple observers of God's commandments shall be rewarded with everlasting life, as obedient children to the heavenly Father. And the transgressors, adders and diminishers of the law of God, shall receive eternal damnation for their just reward. I ask God that we may escape this fearful sentence, and be found such faithful servants and loving children, that we may hear the happy, comfortable, and most joyful sentence, ordained for the children of God, which is: "Come hither, you blessed of my Father, and receive the kingdom of heaven, prepared for you before the beginning of the world."[106]

Unto the Father, the Son, and the Holy Spirit, be all honor and glory, world without end. Amen.

Finis.

---

[106] Matthew 25:34

Colophon

Imprinted at London, in Fleet Street, at the sign of the Sun, over against the Conduit, by Edward Whitchurch, the fifth day of November, in the year of our Lord, 1547.
Cum privileged ad imperilment soul.
(With exclusive rights to print)

For Additional Reading and Study

To learn more about the life and work of Queen Katherine Parr, I recommend the following:

Biographies:

Matzat, Don, *Katherine Parr: The Life and Faith of a Tudor Queen,* KDP Publishing, 2019, 272 pages.
After reading *The Lamentation,* be sure to read my latest work on Queen Katherine. The book contains a biography of her life and faith set within the context of the Reformation. *The Lamentation* is included with a final section "Being Taught by a Queen" in which practical application of her teaching is presented. Katherine Parr was a remarkable woman. Her clear teaching and theology in *The Lamentation* clearly sets forth the basic teachings of the Christian faith.

Linda Porter, *Katherine the Queen: The Remarkable Life of Katherine Parr, the Last Wife of Henry VIII*, St. Martin's Press, 2011, 416 pages.
While this is a good biography. Porter did not appreciate *The Lamentation.* She wrote: "The *Lamentation* has not stood the test of time well. It is neither great literature nor compelling religious writing. No one but a specialist in the period would sit down to read it today. By turns rambling, repetitive and derivative, it is heavily based on St Paul's teachings and epistles." (page 241) I obviously disagree with her assessment. How could one be critical of a theological treatise because it is based on St. Paul's teaching and epistles?

Elizabeth Norton, *Catherine Parr, Wife, Widow, Mother, Survivor, the Story of the Last Queen of Henry VIII,* Amberly Publishing, 2011, 304 pages.
An excellent biography. Regarding the *Lamentation,* Norton wrote: "*The Lamentation of a Sinner* is a remarkable document of Catherine's personal religious beliefs and shows her desire to become a missionary for the Protestant faith."

Anthologies:

Janel Mueller, *Katherine Parr: Complete Works and Correspondence,* University of Chicago Press, 2011, 645 pages. This is a massive scholarly work including Queen Katherine's Correspondence, Personal Prayer Book, Psalms or Prayer and *The Lamentation of a Sinner.*

Brandon G. Winthrow, *Katherine Paar, A Guided Tour of the Life and Thought of a Reformation Queen,* P&R Press, 2009, 187 pages.

Fiction:

Philippa Gregory, *The Taming of the Queen,* Touchstone, 2015, 496 pages.
Like her other novels about Tudor history, this is a fictionalized account of the life of Katherine Parr.

C.J. Sansom, *Lamentation,* Mulholland Books, 2015, 650 pages.
Someone has stolen Queen Katherine's *Lamentation of a Sinner,* placing the life of the Queen in danger, and Detective Shardlake must find the culprit before it's too late.

Tomb of Queen Katherine Parr
at Sudeley Castle in Gloucestershire, England

During the English Civil War St Mary's Church at Sudeley Castle was desecrated and together with the castle was left in ruins. In the years that followed, sightseers visited the church and castle. In 1782 some visiting ladies noticed a panel on the church wall. A local farmer dug under the wall and found a coffin made of lead with the inscription "Here lyeth Quene Kateryn, Wife to Kyng Henry VIII" On opening the coffin it is said the wrapped body was still intact. Queen Katherine had been buried there for over 200 years. It wasn't until 1817 that the open coffin was removed to a stone vault. In 1863 Katherine's remains were put into a new tomb in the newly restored St Mary's Church beneath a marble effigy.

Made in the
USA
Monee, IL